THE ABC OF SNAKES

15 of the most interesting, fun, common and beautiful snakes.

SABAT BEATTO

Dedication

I would like to gratefully to acknowledge the help of P.S. 280 Q students and teachers, who offered their advice and input throughout the writing of this book.

CONTENTS

INTRODUCTION

Snakes are members of the class of animals known as reptiles. Other members of this animal group are lizards, crocodiles, and turtles. Reptiles are cold-blooded, which means their body temperature is the same with that of their environment. This is why they often lie in the sun to raise their body temperature or crawl into the shade to lower the temperature. As the temperature of the environment changes, their body temperature also changes.

There are up to 3000 different species of snakes in the whole world. Snakes can be found almost everywhere: forests, deserts, streams, lakes, and oceans. They can stay on trees, on the ground, and even in water.

Snakes cannot withstand an environment where there is a very low temperature. This is why there are no snakes in Iceland and Antarctica because the place is too cold for them to live. Surprisingly, there are also no snakes in New Zealand, Greenland, and Ireland.

What covers their bodies?

The bodies of snakes are covered with scales. These scales are the reasons why snakes can move over hot or rough surfaces such as the bark of trees, hot sand in the desert and over rocks. Water does not easily pass through the scales because it is waterproof.

Each year, snakes shed a layer of their skin, a few times, and a new layer of skin takes over. When it is time for the skin to be shed, the snake's eye will not be clear and it will not see for a while. This is because it does not have eyelids. To shed this old scale, the snake looks for a rough surface, such as a rock, and runs the old skin against it. This will break the skin very close to the mouth so the snake can easily slide out.

Where do they live?

Snakes can be found in nearly every part of the world except the places I mentioned earlier. They live in grasslands, forests, swamps, and deserts. Many of them live in burrows or spaces in rocks. Some snakes also live partly in water. Snakes do not like the cold because they are cold blooded.

Body size

Snakes have different species, which equally have different sizes. The smallest snake in the world is the thread snake and it is only 10 centimeters or 3.9 inches long. The reticulated python is the longest snake with a length of up to 9 meters or 30 feet, while the largest snake is the green anaconda.

Body description

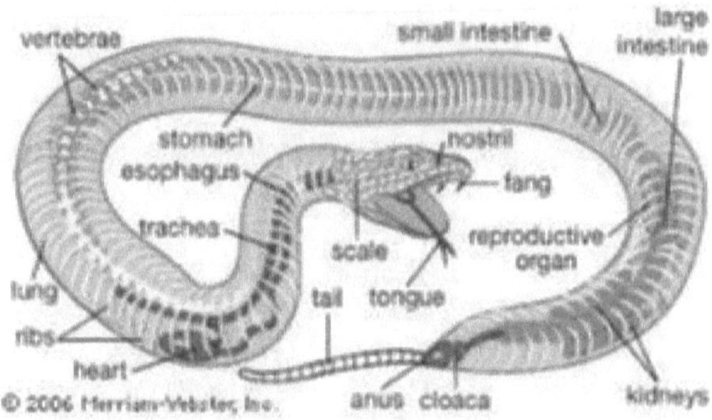

Snakes are vertebrates which means they have bones in their body; although, snakes are very flexible. All the bones and strong muscles in the body of snakes help to protect its internal organs. It has a throat that takes up to one-third of the length of its body. This throat leads to a stomach that is very long. The throat and the stomach can expand to the size of whatever the snake swallows.

The snake also has a long liver, two long lungs, intestines, and kidneys. It also has a long tail.

Movement

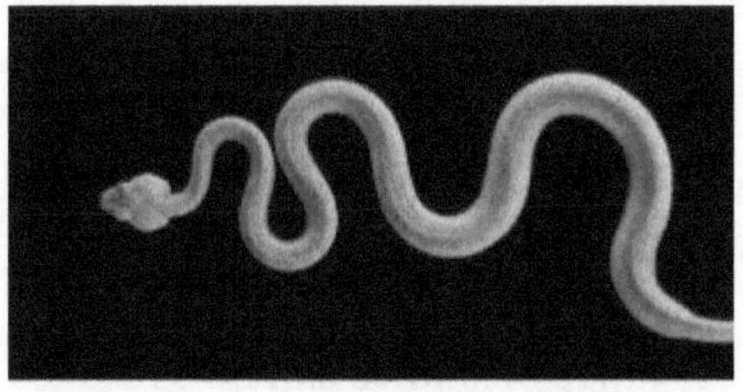

Snakes have no legs. They move by using their scales and muscles. They have four types of movement methods: serpentine, concertina, rectilinear, and sidewinding methods.

Mouth parts

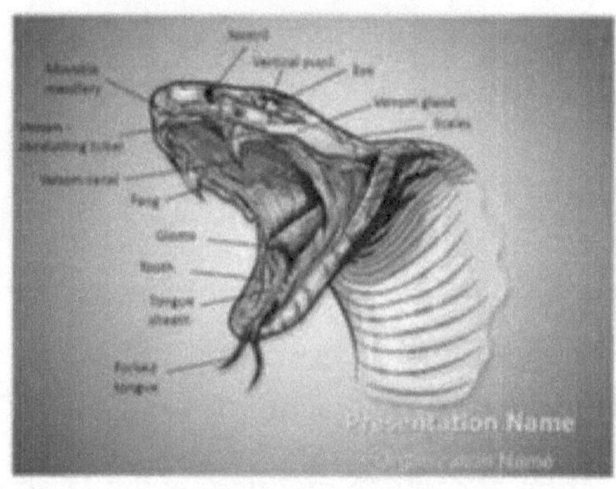

The jaws of humans are fused together at the back of the mouth but those of snakes are not. This is why it is possible for them to swallow big objects, even bigger than their heads because they can stretch the mouths very wide.

Most snakes have teeth but not all of them have fangs. Only venomous snakes have fangs. What are fangs? They are long, sharp and grooved teeth, which are joined to a little bag in the head of the snake. This bag produces a liquid that is poisonous. This poisonous liquid is known as venom. When snakes bite, they release this venom into the body of the prey. This venom will immediately begin to work to either paralyze or kill it.

Examples of venomous snakes are Rattlesnakes, Adders, Cobras, Cottonmouths, and Copperheads. The sea snakes are said to be the most venomous of all snakes.

The venom in the fangs of snakes can be extracted and used to create an antivenin or antivenom, which is used to treat snake bites.

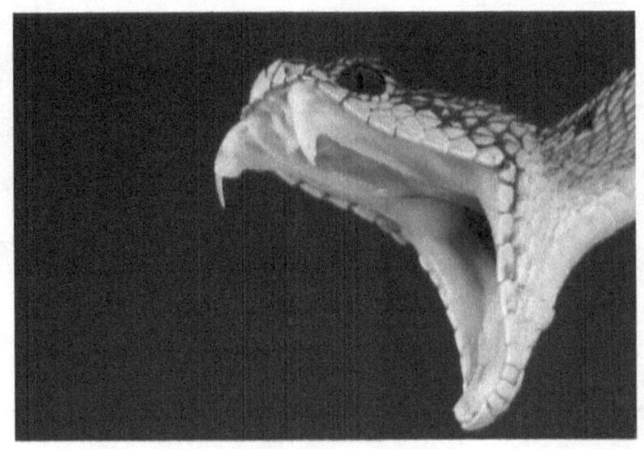

How snakes respond to their environment

Snakes use their senses to escape danger, hunt for food, and to find mates. Snakes generally have poor eyesight but some have keen eyes, while the eyesight of others can only tell the difference between dark and light. Because of this poor eyesight, snakes depend more on their senses of touch and smell.

The noses of snakes are different from those of human beings. They can use them to breathe, but they cannot use them to smell. They smell with their tongues by sticking them out to smell their surroundings.

Snakes have keen senses of detecting vibrations from the environment. They can use the movements of the preys or predators to determine their sizes.

Feeding habits of snakes

Snakes are carnivorous animals, i.e. they can eat only meat. They can eat different types of animals like rodents, termites, frogs, birds, deer, and other reptiles. They can also eat each other. Snakes eat their preys whole, even if they are 3 times bigger than their heads.

While venomous snakes kill their preys by injecting venom into them, constrictors merely squeeze their preys to death. Snakes don't have to hunt for food every day because their rate of metabolism is very slow. Pythons and Anacondas can stay without food for almost one year after eating. Snakes go hunting mostly at nights.

Snakes have strong muscles for swallowing their preys and moving them into their stomachs. After swallowing their preys, snakes release enzymes from their body to break down the food.

Reproduction

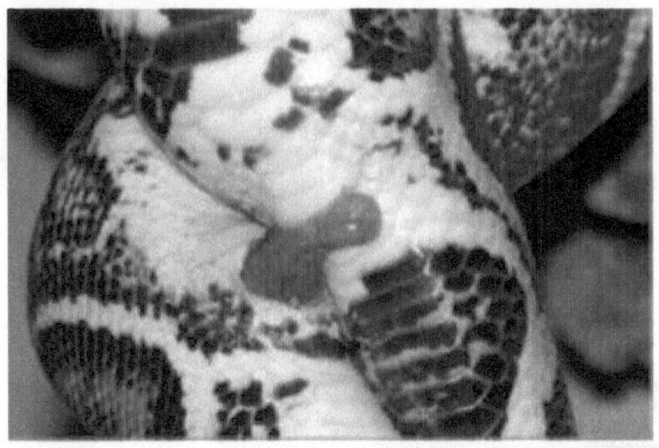

Most species of snakes lay eggs, while some give birth to their young alive. They lay their eggs in warm places. They usually mate in the spring in cold environments but can mate any time of the year in the tropics.

Male snakes try to attract the female by engaging in what is known as "play fighting" with other males who also want the female. The winner of this fight gets to mate with the female.

Snakes give birth once every year to every three years.

Predators

The same way snakes can kill many animals, it is also a target for other animals, i.e. snakes have a lot of enemies who want to eat them. Examples of such enemies are wild boars, large birds, raccoons, mongooses, coyotes, foxes, and even other snakes.

When snakes are young, they are afraid of mammals and birds but when they grow older, they become afraid of human beings.

Snakes have many means of protecting themselves. Some use their body colors as camouflage, some can burrow into the ground. Some use the rattle in their tails to scare off predators. Some will act like they are dead to prevent predators from eating them while some others will try to run away.

Uses of snakes

Human beings use snakes for many things. Some people hunt snakes to eat them. Venomous snakes are hunted so their venom can be extracted to make antivenin or antivenom for saving the lives of those bitten by snakes. The skins of snakes are also used to make things like purses, shoes, and belts. And some just kill snakes because they fear them.

Some facts about snakes

- The heaviest snake is the green anaconda, and it can weigh up to 550 pounds.
- Some species of snakes can live up to 50 years.
- Our fingernails and the scales in the body of snakes are made of the same keratin.
- Cobras learn faster than other snakes.
- Snakes like the Spitting Cobra, the Grass snake, and the Hognose can take their lives to avoid being eaten by predators.
- Some snakes like the paradise tree-snake of Southeast Asia can fly.
- Snakes don't smell with their noses like human beings do, they smell with their tongues.

Snakes have no ears and no eyelids.

Classification/Taxonomy

Kingdom:	Animalia
Subkingdom	Bilateria
Infrakingdom	Deuterostomia
Phylum:	Chordata
Subphylum	Vertebrata
Infraphylum	Gnathostomata
Superclass	Tetrapoda
Class:	Reptilia
Order:	Squamata
Suborder:	Serpentes
Infraorders	Scolecophidia (blind snakes) & Alethinophidia (all others)
Families:	3 in Scolecophidia; 15 in Alethinophidia
Subfamilies	9 in Alethinophidia
Genera	15 in Scolecophidia ; 316 in Alethinophidia
Species	305 in Scolecophidia; 2, 618 in Alethinophidia

Note:- There is no such thing as a poisonous snake. Snakes have venom glands in their mouth where venom is produced. What we have are venomous snakes, not poisonous snakes. A venomous snake can be eaten but poisonous animals, like some salamanders and frogs, cannot be consumed because the poison in their bodies will have your health in a bad way.

For the sake of this book, we are going to talk about 15 of the most interesting, fun, common and beautiful snakes.

PYTHONS

Pythons are found close to the equator, in Africa and Asia, where it is wet and hot, and where they can warm their huge bodies. Wild pythons stay on trees and in caves. Large pythons like to stay on the ground while small pythons climb trees. Sometimes pythons are kept as pets, so they get to live in cities instead of the forests like the wild ones.

All pythons can swim very well. They can eat almost anything that they catch, from livestock like goats, pigs, chickens and cats for those pythons that stay in cities or near them, to lizards, alligators, antelopes, monkeys, deer, wild pigs, etc. for the pythons that live in the wild. They do not attack humans but may do so if they feel threatened by them.

One of the reasons people hunt pythons is for their beautiful, large skins. Python skin is used to make shoes, bags, boots, pants, and vests.

Pythons can grow to a length of between 7 to 30 feet. The longest snake is a python, i.e. the reticulated python. Pythons lay eggs, and have the habit of coiling round the eggs with their body to protect the eggs and also, keep it warm before the eggs hatch.

Examples of well-known pythons are the Burmese python, Green Tree Python, Ball python, Ramsay's python, Myanmar short-tailed python, and the albino ball python.

Where they are found

As said before, pythons are found in Asia, Africa and near the equator. They are also found in Australia and Oceania. Pythons are found in savannahs and deserts, but they prefer the rainforest more. They live in trees, hollows, burrows and under rocks. As some people now use pythons as pets and because places, where they used to stay, are being used by humans to build houses and other things, pythons are now used to staying in cities or near them.

Movement

Because pythons have large body sizes, they move by what is known as rectilinear progression, i.e. movement by sliding forward in a straight line. This form of movement is very slow. The snake will stiffen its ribs, so it acts as support for it against the ground, then the belly is raised upward and the snake pushes itself forward.

They can move in water and on trees.

Feeding habits

According to their sizes, pythons have different types of diets. Small pythons eat lizards, small birds, and rodents. Bigger pythons eat big mammals like wallabies, monkeys, pigs, leopards, and antelopes.

Pythons that live in trees, like the Green Tree Python, will lie still and quiet on a branch of a tree and strike on animals that approach.

Pythons are called Constrictors because they kill their preys by squeezing them to death. They coil themselves around their preys and continue to squeeze them until they can no longer breathe and they die. When these animals stop breathing, pythons swallow them whole. When it is swallowed, the whole animal is digested in the stomach of the python, except the feathers or fur. These fur, feathers or eggshells and beaks are passed out when they excrete. While the food is being digested in the stomach of pythons, they rest in a warm place.

Because digestion is slow in snakes, it takes pythons long periods of time before they digest any food that they swallow. The larger the animals swallowed, the longer the time it will take to digest the food. This is why pythons may eat only 4 or 5 times in a whole year.

Reproduction

Pythons have different mating seasons depending on the species. All pythons lay eggs which means they are oviparous, unlike boas which give birth to their young alive. Many of the species of pythons give parental care to their eggs. Female pythons will make nests using soil and vegetation. The eggs are laid on the nests while the python coils around the eggs to protect them and keep them warm.

Female pythons do not care for their young after they are born. They only care for their eggs.

Lifespan

Pythons can live for over 25 years. Findings show that they can live even up to 35 years.

Interesting Python Facts

- Pythons are one of the largest and heaviest families of snakes.
- Pythons are non-venomous snakes i.e. they do not have venom.
- Pythons are constrictors. This means they kill their prey by squeezing them until they are dead.
- It can take the python weeks or months to digest a prey it has swallowed especially if the prey is big.
- Pythons attack their preys by ambushing them.
- They can camouflage (blend their body color to that of their surroundings) very well and remain undetected by their preys or predators.

- Pythons can locate their preys by sensing the heat in their bodies.
- Female pythons can lay between 12 and 36 eggs.
- The Reticulated Python is the longest snake. It can measure up to 30 feet in length.
- Most pythons weigh between 260 and 300 pounds.
- Pythons move very slowly. On flat ground, it can take a python an hour to move a distance of one mile.
- Pythons come in a lot of colors like brown and green.

ANACONDA

Anacondas are found in the jungles of the Amazon in South America. They are one of the members of the Boa Constrictor family of snakes. They live near lakes, rivers, and swamps. They like to live close to the water so they can easily escape when threatened. Instead of attacking the predator, they will choose to slowly slide into the water so they won't be noticed.

Anacondas eat amphibious animals such as toads and frogs. They also feed on birds, fish, ducks, and turtles. They give birth to their young alive which can be as many as 24 to 35 in number at a time.

Anacondas can grow to incredible sizes of up to 30 feet in length and over 550 pounds in weight with a diameter of more than 12 inches. Female anacondas are larger than the male. The largest snake in terms of weight and length is the Green Anaconda. It is heavier than the reticulated Python in weight but less than it in length. Apart from the Green Anaconda, other varieties are the dark-spotted and the yellow anaconda.

Body description

It is the largest snake in the world but the Reticulated Python is longer in length. It can grow to a length of more than 30 feet and weight of close to 600 pounds.

Feeding

Anacondas feed on large rodents, deer, birds, wild pigs, and aquatic animals like fish, amphibians, and reptiles. Anacondas are good swimmers. They kill their preys by squeezing them to death or by drowning them in water. Anacondas can live without food for years.

They also eat turtles, dogs, sheep, and tapirs. They can also feed on jaguars but an attack on humans is very rare.

They also like to swallow their prey whole by first putting its head in their mouth. Like other snakes, they can swallow animals that are much larger than the size of their head or mouth. While they are feeding, the muscles in the bodies of anacondas crush the animal and help them to push it further into their stomach.

Behavior

The anaconda is a nocturnal animal i.e. it is most active at night. They are non-venomous, so they defend themselves by severely biting their prey or predator but actually kill them by squeezing their body.

Predator

Many people who kill anacondas do so because they are scared and think that they will eat them, but the truth is that anacondas are afraid of humans. Anytime they sense the presence of people, they will run away. It's very rare to see anaconda kill humans. Even jaguars eat anacondas. Anacondas also kill themselves. Piranhas can even kill an anaconda if it's wounded.

Reproduction

Anacondas give birth to their young alive and do not lay eggs. The young anaconda eats rats, frogs, mice, and fish.

Interesting facts about Anaconda

- Anacondas are very hard to find or study, even for scientists.
- They always remain quietly in a position and are hard to trace.
- They spend much of their time in the dark waters of where they live.
- They are amphibious snakes.
- Anacondas are non-venomous. And although they have teeth, they depend on their huge power and body size to kill their victims. They can bite their victims but the bite cannot kill them unless they squeeze them.
- There are local names for anacondas in South America; they are "matatoro" which means killer of bull. They are also called "yukumama" and "sucuri."
- They walk with difficulty on land but are straight and smooth in water and are hard to notice in water.
- Baby anacondas can swim and hunt almost immediately they are born.
- They can live up to 10 years in the wild.

BOA CONSTRICTOR

The Boa Constrictors are the most beautifully colored snakes in the world. They are also one of the largest, along with the Anaconda and Reticulated Python. Boas are deadly snakes although they are non-venomous. They catch their preys by ambush, which means they give their preys surprise attack by hiding in a place and waiting for them to appear and then attacking them suddenly. After catching their prey, they coil around them and squeeze until they are not able to breathe and then dies.

They can eat lizards, birds, small mammals, and frogs. Boas that are very big can eat big animals like deer, monkeys, and pigs. They have scales that are sensitive to heat which they use to search for prey when it gets dark.

Boas live in tropical South and Central America. They like hot places and can be found on trees and on the ground. Boas do not lay eggs but give birth to their young alive. Their young completely develop inside the female. When they are born, they immediately learn to take care of themselves.

Boas are also good swimmers like anaconda but prefer staying on dry land.

Boa constrictors are in great demands because of their colorful and beautiful skins which are used to make bags, shoes, jackets, etc.

Body description and size

They have very beautiful markings on their bodies. They can blend into their surroundings by using different colors like red, yellow, or green.

The boa constrictor can grow to a size of 13 feet or 4 meters in length and can weigh up to 45 kilograms or 100 pounds.

Where they live

Boa constrictors can be found anywhere from South to Central America. They are also found off the coast of the Pacific and on Caribbean islands. They are known as New World snakes because they live exclusively in the Western hemisphere.

They can be found in rainforests, woodlands, semi-deserts, and dry tropical deserts, etc. They tend to live near rivers or streams.

How they behave

They are typically solitary animals. They mostly come out at night and sometimes in the day to enjoy the sun when the temperature is not too high.

They move in straight lines instead of the back and forth slithering. They also shed their skin to grow as all snakes do. Boa constrictors have very good vision. They can also use their tongues to sense things.

What they eat and how they hunt for food

Like I said before, a boa constrictor will ambush its prey. They also eat small and big animals like squirrels, rats, and pigs, monkeys, deer. Their favorite food is bats.

They have hooked teeth which are small; for grabbing and holding their prey. If their teeth are damaged or fall out, they can grow them again. They have no fangs.

Reproduction

Boas tend to do things alone but come together when it's time to mate. They commonly mate during the dry season. Their males mate every year while their females do not. The females can mate with one or more male in a season. Females are scattered over a wide area and it is the work of males to find them. The female help the male to find them by releasing a scent so the male can use it to track them. They release this scent when they are ready to mate.

As said before, boa constrictors give birth to live young, which makes them ovoviviparous. The time between mating and giving birth is between 5 and 8 months. The average number of young given birth to is around 25. They can give birth to between 10 and 64 young.

Young boa constrictors spend most of their time in trees but will spend more time on the ground when they become heavier and larger. It takes between 2 or 3 years for a boa constrictor to mature sexually and be ready to give birth or mate.

Interesting facts about boa constrictors

- Boa constrictors do not attack people unless they want to protect themselves from people who want to kill them.
- They are the most beautiful snakes with interesting prints and colorful skin.

- Boa constrictors are placed on the list of endangered animals because people were killing them in large numbers for their attractive and colorful skin.
- The hooked teeth of the Boa Constrictors are not used for chewing but for catching prey.
- They provide camouflage, i.e. change their body color and design to those of their surroundings.
- They are cold-blooded animals and have something that they use to detect their warm-blooded prey. They can also use the taste of smell on their tongues to find their preys.
- Because the boa constrictor is an excellent hunter, South Americans use them to eradicate pests, like rodents.
- Boa constrictors are solitary animals.
- Boa constrictors can live up to 20 or 30 years in the wild.

COBRAS

Cobras are some of the most recognized and widely known snakes in the world. They are particularly famous for their upright postures which are very threatening and their equally threatening hoods. They are feared and respected because of their venomous bite, their prideful posture, and their elegance. "Cobra" is taken from a Portuguese word which means "hooded snake."

Cobras are found in the Middle East, Africa, Australia, Southeast Asia, India, and Indonesia. The Coral Snakes which are relatives of the Cobras are found in the US. Cobras can be found in trees, underground, and under rocks. They live in forests near streams.

There are up to 270 different Cobra types and they have relatives like Adders, Taipans, Mambas, etc. They all have short fangs and are extremely venomous.

Cobras, unlike boa constrictor, lay eggs. They stay around their eggs to defend them until they hatch. Mongooses and Wild Boars like to steal Cobra eggs. The Mongoose is not an easy animal for Cobras to kill because they are agile and fast. Their thick fur also protects them from the venomous fangs of the Cobra.

The Spitting Cobra has a unique talent which is its ability to spit out venom to a distance of more than 6 feet. Not only can this snake spit its venom over a long distance, but it also has an accurate aim. It always aims the prey's eyes. Cobra's venom in the eyes can lead to blindness if it's not washed well.

Body description and behavior
Cobras have hollow fangs which are fixed to the upper jaws close to the front of their mouths. Because Cobras cannot hold down preys using their fangs, they inject them with their venom through their fangs.

Cobras have different varieties with different colors of black, red, yellow, and many other patterns and colors.

Cobras are popular because of the threatening hood at their necks. When they are angry or feel threatened, they spread out their hoods. Cobras are able to raise their heads high up off the ground. This helps them to search for food even from far distances and make them threatening to predators. They can also make a loud hissing sound to scare away potential predators.

Size

Cobras are large snakes. The Mozambique Spitting Cobra with a length of about 4 feet is the smallest Cobra species. The largest true Cobra is the forest Cobra with around 10 feet length. The largest Cobra in the world is the Asher's Spitting Cobra which is about 9 feet. The King Cobra is the longest venomous snake on earth and it can measure up to 18 feet in length.

Where they are found

They are commonly found in tropical, hot areas but also live in grasslands, savannahs, farming areas and forests in Southern Asia and Africa. They enjoy spending time in trees, underground and under rocks.

Reproduction

They can lay eggs to produce young ones, unlike some snakes that give birth to live young. They can lay between 20 and 40 eggs at a time. The incubation period (the practice of sitting on eggs by female Cobras to warm them so they can hatch) is 60 to 80 days. They will stay very close to the eggs and protect them until they hatch.

Predators

The most well-known enemy of Cobras isthe Mongoose. Because the mongoose is protected against Cobra's venomous bite as a result of their thick fur, they often defeat the Cobra in fights. They are also faster and are more agile. They are so fast that they will bite the Cobra's back before it even protects itself. Man and other snakes are also threatto the Cobra.

The mongoose and the wild boar use to steal Cobra's eggs.

What they eat and how they hunt for food

Cobras are good hunters. They will follow their preys quietly until they are ready to attack. They can run very fast even when their heads are raised. They can eat other snakes i.e. they are cannibals. They can also eat small mammals, eggs of birds, and birds. Most Cobras hunt for food at night but some species hunt even in the heat of the day.

Their metabolism is slow, just like other snakes. They can stay without food for weeks or months after they've eaten.

Cobra's bite

Cobra bites can cause the death of the person who is bitten especially if the bite is not treated. Luckily, there are antivenin or anti-venom that can be used to save the person's life. The bite of a cobra contains neurotoxins, i.e. the venom released during the bite affects the nervous system. A person bitten by a Cobra will not be able to breath, speak, see, swallow, walk or move the body very well. The person may experience respiratory failure, abdominal pain, vomiting, etc.

A person bitten by a Cobra may die within 30 minutes if he is not treated.

Interesting facts about Cobras

- Cobras can be used by snake charmers to entertain people.
- Cobras produce a large volume of venom. In just a single bite, a large elephant can be killed.
- Cobras feed on birds, mammals, frogs, fish, lizards, and other snakes.
- They swallow their prey whole, like other snakes.
- A quiver is a group of Cobras.
- They are the only snakes that exhibit parental behavior of building a nest for their eggs and protecting them until they hatch.
- Female Cobras can lay up to 40 eggs.
- They can live up to 20 years in the wild.

RATTLESNAKES

The rattlesnake is well-known for its rattle. Rattlesnake babies have what can be called a pre-button when they are born. The first time the baby rattlesnake sheds its skin, it loses this pre-button. After the shedding, a new button appears. Every other time that the snake shed its skin, another button or rattle is added, so that the number of button or rattle increases.

These buttons are made up of the same material that scales and fingernails are made of, which is keratin. The noise made by the rattles are as a result of the knocking together of segments of the rattle. This is why a rattle will only make a sound when it consists of more than one piece.

Rattlesnakes can be found all through South and North America. The biggest collection of rattlesnakes in the world can be found in the southern parts of the United States and in Northern Mexico. There are up to 13 species of rattlesnakes in Arizona alone. They can be found in the mountains and deserts and can grow to 3 or 4 feet in length.

Examples of rattlesnakes are Western Diamondback, Eastern Diamondback, Speckled, Sidewinder, etc. They are all venomous and have rattles.

Rattlesnakes eat squirrels, rabbits, rodents, and other small critters. They hibernate i.e. sleep or rest during the winter then come out to feed and mate in the spring.

Rattle and hiss

The rattlesnake has an extremely effective warning sign with which it scares away predators. The rattle is a very sophisticated and highly effective warning system.

The second element of the rattlesnake's warning posture is the hiss. The hiss is often overshadowed and overlooked by the rattle. When a rattlesnake is threatened, it hisses and rattles its tail as a warning sign.

Size and body description

Rattlesnakes have different sizes that range from 1 to 8 feet. They have thick bodies and scales in different patterns and colors. Rattlesnakes have a distinctive triangular head, apart from their rattle. They also have eyes like those of cats.

Baby and young rattlesnakes may not have their rattle yet, but they are as dangerous as their adults. Some adult rattlesnakes may also have lost their rattles, so another way to identify them is their triangular head.

Habitat

This snake can survive in a lot of places. Though there are more of them in the desert sands of the Southwest, they are also found in scrub bushes, rocky hills, grasslands, etc. They live in the meadows of the Northeast and the swamplands of the Southeastern United States.

Behavior

Rattlesnakes are known to spend time in dens. Generations of rattlesnakes can use the same dens. They can use the same den for over 100 years. Rattlesnakes enjoy sunning their bodies on open places like rocks after leaving their dens. They are not nocturnal snakes like the Cobras.

Predators

Even with their strong venom, rattlesnakes cannot kill king snakes. These snakes eat rattlesnakes. One of the snakes that are not affected by the venom or bite of rattlesnakes is the king snake, this is why it is the major predator of rattlesnakes.

Reproduction

They do not lay eggs in nests but instead give birth to live young because they are ovoviviparous. Their females can reproduce once in a two-year period and carry the eggs in their bodies for close to 3 months. They can give birth to about 10 baby rattlesnakes or rattlers. Young rattlesnakes begin to fend for themselves almost immediately they are born. These snakes can live up to 25.

Feeding

Their favorite foods are lizards and small rodents. They like to ambush their prey and strike them when they are close. Their venom paralyzes the prey which is then swallowed whole. They like to hide after eating because they become sluggish by then.

Bite

Rattlesnakes don't commonly bite humans unless they step on them or attack them. Their bite can be dangerous even though it may not kill them. With proper treatment, their bites may not be serious to humans.

Rattlesnakes' venom has a very strong and powerful effect. When bitten, humans can experience permanent or temporary muscle or tissue damage or both, internal bleeding, loss of the part of the body where the bite happened, serious and severe pain around the area.

The venom of some rattlesnakes affects the nervous system.

Interesting fact about Rattlesnake:

- The average size of rattlesnakes is 3 or 4 feet. The largest species can be up to 8 feet in length.
- They are commonly brown, grey, black or olive in color, so they are not that colorful.
- They are fond of blending with their surroundings.
- They have triangular heads
- Their rattle is made of keratin just like our fingernails and hairs.
- They can sometimes give what is known as "dry bites." This involves biting without releasing venom.
- Their bites can be fatal for humans if treatment is delayed or not given
- They are carnivores. They usually eat rats, small birds, mice.
- Rattlesnakes are the most evolved and newest snakes in the whole world

ADDER

The term "Adder" is an Old English word which means serpent. Nearly all the adders are venomous snakes but not all of them are dangerous to humans. There are many snakes whose names contain the word "adder" but there is only one snake with the single name of the adder. The adder is also known as a black adder, common adder, common European adder or common European viper. It is commonly found in nearly all of Western Europe and East Asia. It is the only venomous snake belonging to Britain.

Description and size

Adders are small when compared to other snakes. The average length of adult adders is around 24 inches. They also have thick bodies.

Adders are commonly reddish-brown or gray in color; they can also be white, black, pale yellow or cream. On the heads of adders, you will find a V shape, they also have their eyes partially covered with scales making it look like their eyes are blocked or covered. Female adders are known to be browner and redder than males, while the males have black, gray and white coloration. Females are also larger.

Their fangs are hinged making it possible for them to grow very long. Their venom is released through these fangs.

Where they live

They are shy snakes that like to live alone. They prefer the ground to trees. They are usually seen during sunset when they go in search of food.

They are found in open countryside and on the edge of the woods. They like dunes or open meadows for sunning themselves and scrub leaves and rocks. They are not common in urban areas.

What they eat and how they hunt for food

Adders mostly eat small mammals. They also eat frogs, lizards, and nesting birds. When adders identify their preys, they strike at them and inject their venom into them. They release these preys almost immediately so they don't bite them back. They allow the prey to go but go after them by using their sense of smell to find them after they might have died from the venom in their body.

Reproduction

The males search for the females by using their sense of smell. They sometimes fight for these females. After mating, the females look for a good place to give birth.

Adders are ovoviviparous, so they give birth to live young. Pregnancy is 3 to 4 months. They usually give birth to about 12 babies.

These babies are normally about 7 inches and look very much like adult snakes. They take 3 to 4 years to mature and can live up to 15 years.

Bite

Although adders are venomous and have the best-developed mechanism of injecting venom, they are not aggressive and only bite if threatened. Their venom is not that poisonous but anybody bitten still needs to be treated. When bitten, the person can experience drowsiness, nausea, bruising and swelling in the area of the bite.

It's better to treat adders with respect and leave them alone because most of the people bitten by adders were trying to handle them.

Predators

Predators like adult snakes and the common buzzard are threats to young adders. They are also killed by rodents when they are in hibernation.

Interesting facts about adders

- The adder is the only venomous snake native to England.
- They are usually found in grasslands, swamps, wetlands, forests, semi-deserts and rocky slopes.
- Their venom is used in traditional medicine.
- Adders can easily locate their prey.
- The strength of their venom is medium i.e. it can kill small animals but not humans. It can cause nausea, diarrhea, and drowsiness in the person. Medical treatment is normally required.
- They are carnivores. They feed on animals like lizards, mice, frogs, newts, insects, and small birds.
- They like to sun themselves because they are cold-blooded
- Adders go on hibernation in the winters.
- When females are ready to mate, they release a specific smell which the males use to search for them.

- Babies are born only once in 3 years and pregnancy is 3 or 4 month

COPPERHEAD

Copperheads are very common in North America. Even though the strength of their venom is mild, they are very likely to bite. They get their name from their copper-red heads. Some other snakes are called copperheads but only the North American copperhead has its scientific name while it's a common name for the others.

Copperheads have the ability to sense or detect a very small change in temperature. This helps them to track and hunt preys.

Description and size

They have medium sizes of between 2 and 3 feet length. Male copperheads are shorter than females but have longer tails. They have bodies with unique patterns. These patterns have reddish-brown cross-bands that are shaped like an hourglass or dumbbell.

There are many snakes with patterns and colors similar to those of copperheads and so are usually mistaken for copperheads. But the only snakes with hourglass-shaped markings are copperheads.

Where they are found

Copperheads are found from Northern Mexico and West Texas to Southern New England. They like mountains, woods, rocky areas, canyons, and other natural surroundings. They can live in almost any place so far it has sunlight and cover.

They like to hide under surface covers like metal sheets, boards, flat rocks, and logs. So they can be found in junkyards, abandoned farm buildings, piles of sawdust and wood and old construction areas.

Characteristics

Copperheads use camouflage to protect themselves. They are more prone to bite at night when they are on the move than when they are resting during the day. When they are annoyed or bothered, they will rapidly shake their tails and release musk of strong smell.

They are semi-social snakes which is why copperheads hunt alone but hibernate in communal dens. They can be seen eating, drinking, courting and basking in the sun together.

They are nocturnal in the summer but go about during the day in the spring and fall. Although they normally stay on the ground, they sometimes climb low trees and bushes to look for prey or put themselves in the sun.

What they eat and how they hunt for food:

They love to eat small rodents and birds, small snakes, lizards, salamanders, frogs, and some large insects. They like to ambush their preys but sometimes go in search of them using their ability to sense heat or a rise in temperature.

When a large prey is attacked, the prey is bitten and then released after its venom has been deposited in the prey. They give time for the venom to work on the prey and then track them down once they are dead. If it was a smaller prey, copperheads will hold them in their mouths until they die. They eat between 10 or 12 times a year.

More people are bitten by copperheads in America than any other species of snakes and luckily, the strength of the venom is mild. Copperheads strike almost instantly without any warning sign if they feel threatened, unlike most venomous snakes.

Reproduction

Copperheads' mating season, which can be dramatic, begins in February and ends in May and also begins in August and ends in October. Males engage in ritual fights in the presence of a female to win her attention. Females also sometimes engage in combat with prospective mates, and will always refuse to accept males who reject their challenge.

Their babies are born live because they are ovoviviparous. Baby copperheads are born with both venom and fangs and they mostly feed on insects like caterpillars.

Interesting facts about copperheads

- There is a relation between the length of copperheads and their fangs. The shorter or longer the snake, the longer or shorter the fangs.
- Copperheads sometimes release musk when they are touched.
- An enzyme extracted from the venom of copperheads has the ability to prevent the growth of cancer.
- Copperheads have amazing camouflage, making it difficult to detect them.

Garter Snakes

The garter snake is one of the most well-known snakes in Canada. They are found everywhere in Canada and in the central parts of America. Their average length is 60 to 80 cm i.e. 23-30 inches and they can grow to a length of 135 cm.

They are very small and are often kept as pets. Although some species have venom with mild strength, they are relatively harmless.

They hibernate in winter because they live in colder temperatures. They stay in cracks in the ground where the frost hasn't gotten to. You can find as much as 100 garter snakes gathered together in a place. They majorly feed on earthworms, leeches, fish, tadpoles, frogs, and sometimes mice. Some of their many predators are bears, skunks, raccoons, crows and hawks.

They give birth to their young, live. The average number of babies born at a time is usually between 20 and 40, 98 being the highest.

Description and size

They have a variety of colors but most of them have 3 longitudinal stripes. They are usually small with an average length of 23 to 30 inches but some may grow up to 5 feet. Many species of garter snakes have two colors in their tongues.

Where they are found

They live in meadows, Woodlands, and grassy knolls. They like to live near water. Garter snakes are found throughout North America, from the Pacific Ocean and Southern Canada to the Atlantic Ocean.

They are very common in the US and they are the most popular reptiles in Massachusetts.

Characteristics

They move really fast and are active during the day. They live mostly on the ground but some may climb vines or shrubs. Some garter snake species are very good swimmers.

They release foul-smelling musk when threatened. Their small size makes them more likely to be eaten by predators like hawks, bullfrogs, foxes, squirrels, etc.

What they feed on and how they hunt

Garter snakes mostly eat amphibians, fishes, and earthworms. They use their sharp teeth to render their preys motionless. The saliva of some species has neurotoxin which paralyzes the prey. This makes it easier to swallow the prey.

Although the bite of many of them is harmless because they are non-venomous, this bite can cause itching and swelling in humans.

Reproduction

Garter snakes mate best when they are gathered together in a place and are about going into hibernation and also after coming out from it.

Female garter snakes release chemicals to attract males. Dozens of males can come for one female. This type of mating is known as "mating ball."

They give birth to live young because they are ovoviviparous. They give birth to between 20 and 40 babies at a time.

Interesting facts about garter snake

- Garter snakes are mistakenly called garden snakes because of the similar sounding pronunciation.
- They are harmless snakes but defend themselves when threatened.
- They are the most well-known snakes in North America.
- They hibernate together in large numbers.
- The best way to get rid of garter snakes is to leave them alone because they are harmless.

Black Mamba

The black mamba is the second largest venomous snake on earth. It's fast, highly aggressive when threatened, nervous, and lethally venomous. They are in the top list of the most venomous snakes in the world and are responsible for many human deaths. The above-mentioned qualities of black mambas make them the world's deadliest snakes.

They can grow up to a length of 14 feet. The name black mamba is not gotten from the color of their skins but from the color of the roof of their mouths.

They are found in Eastern and Southern Africa. They live in Eritrea, Namibia, South Africa, etc. Apart from its speed of around 12 miles in one hour, it is also a fast climber. It can also live up to 12 years in captivity.

It can bite its target many times in a short period of time. It likes to attack its prey in the head. The black mamba can rise up to a height of around 4 feet.

Description

The black mamba can be gray, brown khaki or olive in color but not black. Its average length is between 2 and 3 meters but can grow up to 4.5 meters. They are one of the fastest snakes on earth.

Bite

The bite from black mamba can easily kill a man. The deadly venom takes around 30 minutes to 3 hours to kill the person. Bites from black mamba can cause vital body organs to stop working. The venom in the bites is so strong that sometimes, even the antivenin or antivenom will not be strong enough to cure the person. It's really a dangerous snake.

Well, known places where black mambas live are Ethiopia, Somalia, Kenya, Republic of Congo, etc. They can live almost anywhere as far as they get what they need. They live in swamps, forests, woods, and the savannah. Wherever the black mambas decide the live, it's always very difficult to send them out, i.e. they are possessive.

What they eat and how they hunt for food

They eat small mammals such as squirrels and rodents. They sometimes feed on birds. They bite their prey once or twice and patiently wait for them to die or become paralyzed. Food digests in their stomachs faster than most snakes. It takes between 8 and 10 hours for digestion to take place.

Predators

Some of the animals that prey on black mambas are mongooses, crocodiles, birds of prey, jackals, foxes, etc. Humans kill them because of fear of their venomous bites.

Behavior

Black mambas are shy animals. They like to live alone and avoid other animals, but become aggressive if threatened or confronted. When threatened, they raise their heads, expand their hoods with their mouths opened and tongues flicking. They will also hiss. They bite fast and many times within a short time. They also like to enjoy themselves in the sun.

Reproduction

Black mambas don't associate or relate with themselves before mating. After mating, the male and the female go back to their places. It takes 2 to 3 months from the time of mating for the female to lay eggs. The numbers of eggs are between 6 and 17. It also takes 2 to 3 months for the eggs to hatch. After hatching, the female puts the eggs in a safe place and leaves. They do not provide any form of care for the newly hatched snakes. The baby mambas have to start defending themselves immediately they are hatched.

Interesting facts about Black mamba:

- They are long snakes which can reach a length of 12 feet and a weight of 3.5 pounds.
- Black mambas are known to display their black mouths when in danger.
- When they are ready to attack, they flatten their necks and hiss.
- Even with their bad reputation of being deadly, black mambas will first try to run away when they see human beings. They will only attack when they feel threatened.
- Their venom is so strong that it can kill anybody bitten in less than 20 minutes.

- They live in crevices of rocks and holes in trees.
- They are diurnal animals i.e. they are active in the day.
- They move very fast. They can cover a distance of 12 miles in one hour.
- Female black mambas are the ones who choose the males to mate with.
- After mating, females become very aggressive and often chase their partners away.
- They can live up to 12 years in captivity and 11 years in the wild.

COTTONMOUTH

Cottonmouth snakes, like all pit vipers (rattlesnakes, copperheads), possess pits on their faces. These pits help them to sense heat in their surroundings, making it easy for them to detect the presence of both preys and predators. The cottonmouth snakes are also called the water moccasin, black moccasin, water mamba, black snake, water pilot, mangrove rattler, etc. The snake is named cottonmouth because its mouth resembles cotton when it's open. They are the only venomous water snakes in North America.

They have an easily distinguishable triangular and blocky head, a dangerous bite, and a thick body. Like most snakes, they don't bite humans unless threatened. They can live both on land and in water. The Southeastern United States is their native range.

Description and size

They are of average size, with the length of between 2 and 4 feet. They have a variety of colors like black, dark brown, olive, yellow, etc. They have bellies that are lighter in color than their backs.

Where they live

Cottonmouths can be found in Southern Virginia, Eastern Texas, and Florida. They can be seen in marshes, swamps, ditches, edges of lakes, streams, and ponds. They are found near water, even when they are on land. They like to bask in the sun to raise the temperature of their body.

What they eat and how they hunt for food

They work during the day and also at night, but they majorly hunt when it's dark. They feed on small mammals, fish, amphibians, birds, reptiles like baby alligators, lizards, turtles, and other snakes.

Reproduction

Cottonmouths mate in spring. During the mating process, the males move around and wave their tails as a way of luring females from other suitors. Male cottonmouths also fight themselves to win the attention of their females.

They don't lay eggs but give birth to live young because they are ovoviviparous. They give birth once every 2 or 3 years to between 10 and 20 cottonmouth baby snakes. The pregnancy lasts for 3 or 4 months. Parents don't provide any care after their baby is born.

Behaviors

Cottonmouths are known to be aggressive but will only attack humans on provocation. The difference between them and other water snakes is that they will stand and face the threat while nonvenomous water snakes will run away.

Cottonmouths, when they feel threatened, will coil their bodies and open their mouths to show the white color in their tongues. This habit of opening their mouths is a warning signal to predators.

Bite

The venom of cottonmouth snakes is very strong. Their venom contains an agent that prevents the blood from clotting. This causes people bitten by these snakes to bleed for a long time. It can also cause serious pain around the area where the person was bitten. It can cause muscle damage, internal bleeding, etc.

Interesting facts about cottonmouths

- The most common snake in Florida is the cottonmouth.
- The male cottonmouth is larger than the female.
- Cottonmouth snakes are commonly found near water bodies like ponds, swamps, the edge of lakes, slow-moving streams, etc.
- When it's threatened, the cottonmouth will stand up and opens its mouth. This is done to warn or scare away predators.
- The venom of cottonmouths is more toxic than that of the Copperheads but less than that of rattlesnakes and other vipers.
- Cottonmouth can sometimes give a "dry bite", i.e. bite without releasing venom into the body of the animal or human being.
- When compared to other venomous snakes in North America, the cottonmouth venom is not that strong and may not be able to kill an adult human but can cause serious pain, loss of limbs or digits, and gangrene if the bite is not adequately treated.

CORAL

Coral snakes are highly venomous, small in size and vibrantly colored. They have very deadly venom even though they are not as strong as that of the black mamba. Even with their very strong venom, they are not considered to be as dangerous as rattlesnakes because their system of delivering venom through their bite is not that effective when compared to that of rattlesnakes.

Coral snakes can be divided into 2 groups: the Old World coral snakes which can be found in Asia and the New World coral snakes which can be found in the Americas. New World coral snakes are some of the most venomous snakes in North America.

Description and size

Coral snakes have an average length of between 20 and 30 inches. They have brilliant colors which consist of red, yellow and black bands. They have small heads. They also have small fangs which are why it's more difficult for coral snakes to deliver venom to their victims, for instance, through a thick leather jacket, as compared to other snakes who have large fangs and so can easily deliver their venom.

Behavior

They are nocturnal snakes i.e. active at night and stay hidden in the daytime. They are not aggressive snakes. When faced with human beings, they normally run away and will only bite as the last option if threatened.

Because their venom is not that strong, their bite can often lead to mild pain, double vision, slurred speech, muscular paralysis and can overwhelm the respiratory system leading to cardiac arrest if the bite is left untreated.

Since antivenin was introduced in America in 1967, there has not been a record of a single death related to coral snake bite.

They live in jungles or forests and spend a lot of time hidden in leaf piles, in tree stumps, under rocks or in underground burrows. They like to stay in swamps, wooded and marshy areas.

They are shy snakes and will often run away from predators, especially humans. They may be found in suburban areas because of their secretive habits.

What they eat and how they hunt for food

Coral snakes hunt and eat snakes, even coral snakes, which is why they are called ophiophagous. They also eat insects, mice, lizards, small birds, and frogs. After their prey is paralyzed by their venom, they swallow them whole.

Their fangs are weak compared to other venomous snakes. Because of their weak and small fangs, it's hard for them to puncture human skin with their bite, not to talk of leather jackets. When they bite animals, they try to hold on to them for some time because they don't have much venom in their fangs.

Reproduction

The coral snake is the only North American venomous snake that lay eggs. Eggs are laid in the summer. It takes between 2 and 3 months for the eggs to hatch.

Interesting Facts about Coral Snakes

- They cannot move their fangs into their mouths. When they are not in use, their fangs are always in an upright position.
- They can live up to 7 years in captivity but their average lifespan in the wild is not known.
- They are closely related to Mambas, Cobras and sea snakes.
- They are small in length with the average length of 18 to 20 inches. They can grow to a length of 3 feet.
- Because the tail and the head of the coral snake are similar, when threatened, they curl together and display their tail to confuse predators.
- They are nocturnal snakes, i.e. they are active at night.
- They are not aggressive and would rather run away than stand up to predators.
- They are carnivores, i.e. they eat meat, even feeding on coral snakes and other snakes.
- They are the only North American venomous snakes that lay eggs; others give birth to live young.

FLYING SNAKE

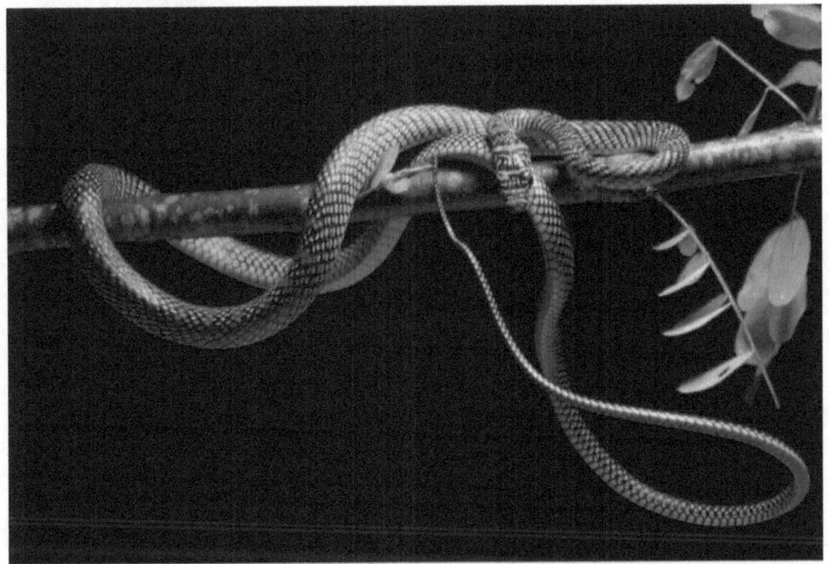

Chrysopelea which is known as the gliding snake and more commonly as the flying snake is a family of mildly venomous snakes. They are found in South and Southeast Asia i.e. Malaysia, Indonesia, China, India, Philippines, Sri Lanka, Singapore, Laos, Thailand, Vietnam, and Cambodia. These snakes can glide from tree to tree. Apart from their ability to fly from tree to tree, they are also very good climbers.

Description and Size:
Flying snakes are small in size with a maximum growth of 4 feet. Adult flying snakes have slender bodies and long tails.

Most of them have yellow scales on their backs; some have a stripe of red scales. Their adults have bright yellow scales on their abdomens.

Where they live

They are arboreal animals i.e. they live on trees, and do not like to come down from them. They are found in different types of places like gardens, parks, forests, and jungles. They like staying on top of coconut palms, especially in Singapore.

How they fly:

In moving from one tree to another, flying snakes simply glide through the air and not the typical flying of birds. They do not have wings so they can only glide through the air. They climb trees using the ridge scales on their abdomen. They push their bodies against the rough bark surface of tree trunks, making it possible for them to move up vertically on a tree. They continue in this movement until they get to the end of a branch of a tree, where they wrap their tails around the branch and dangle it. It decides on where it wants to land, and then pushes its body forward, away from the tree and safely lands on its target tree. To be able to fly, the flying snake turns its body into a false wing by tightening its abdomen and spreading out its ribs. In this form, it's able to make a continuous curving and twisting motion.

They can glide better than even flying squirrels, even though they do not possess wings, limbs or any other projections that look like wings.

Flying snakes can glide at a fast speed of more than 30 feet per second. They can travel a distance of up to 330 feet in the air.

What they eat and how they hunt for food

Flying snakes are diurnal animals, i.e. they are active during the day. Their main source of food is lizards that live on trees. They also feed on frogs, rodents, bats, and birds.

They have fangs that are fixed to the back of their mouths. These fangs are used to release venom to the body of the prey when they bite. Their venom is mild in strength so it's only strong enough to paralyze small preys. Their venom is harmless to humans.

Interesting facts about flying snakes
- Flying snakes can alter the shape of their bodies so they can fly.
- Scientists are planning to use the knowledge of how flying snakes move through the air to create robots which can glide from place to place in the air.

- They don't just land anyway. Before they begin gliding, they first decide where to land.
- There are 5 species of flying snakes distributed between Indonesia and India.
- They almost never leave the top of trees because they are strongly arboreal.
- They escape from predators by flying away.
- They are carnivorous snakes.
- Flying snakes cannot fly upwards. They can only fly from a higher spot or position on one tree to a lower position on another tree.
- There's no record of flying snakes landing on people.

Krait

The common krait which is also known as the blue krait or Indian krait is one of the 4 most venomous snakes in India.

Description and size

Their average length is 3 feet but can grow to a length of 6 feet. Male kraits are longer than the females. They also have longer tails.

They have flat heads and necks that is almost never seen. They have cylindrical bodies which increasingly become reduced till they get to the tail. They have round and short tails. They have small eyes with round pupils.

They are generally bluish black or black in color with white crossbars. They have their bellies and upper lips in white colors.

Where they live

They are found in India, Pakistan, Sri Lanka, Bangladesh, Nepal, and Afghanistan. They can be found in different habitats like fields, jungles, and even inhabited places. They are known to live in rat holes, brick poles, termite mounds, and even inside houses. They live in water or near it.

What they eat and how they hunt for food:
They feed mainly on other snakes and other kraits, even their young. They also eat small mammals (like mice and rats), frogs, and lizards. Young kraits eat arthropods.

Behavior:

There's a great difference in behavior between the night and the daytime for kraits. They are generally docile and sluggish. They hide in loose soil, rodent holes, under debris, and are rarely seen. They commonly roll their bodies into a coiled, loose ball, and keep their heads well hidden. In this condition, the snake can be handled to a certain extent, and will only bite when they're over handled.

They are very active at night and escape from predators by remaining motionless and acting "dead" or making a loud hissing noise.

When disturbed or threatened, they coil up with their heads hidden and their bodies flattened while also making jerky movements. They may also raise their tails. They don't like to bite but when they do, they normally cling to their prey for some time so they can inject a considerable quantity of venom into them. They may be aggressive at night when disturbed or threatened.

Venom:

Kraits have very strong venom which can cause paralysis. A lot of people may take a krait bite for granted because little or no pain occurs when bit but this does not mean that its bite isn't dangerous. Symptoms begins with the tightening of muscles of the face in less than 2 hours after the bite, then sharp pain in the abdomen, inability to speak or see, and gradual paralysis, leading to death.

Bite from kraits can sometimes lead to death. Between 4 to 8 hours after being bitten, if the bite isn't treated it can lead to death. If the victim was sleeping when he was being bitten, he may not notice it because the bite will feel like that of mosquito or ant. He may never wake up. The victims are always suffocated to death. One way of detecting krait bite is that it produces little swelling around the affected part.

Interesting facts about krait snake:
- They lay eggs in clutches of between 2 and 14.
- They like to feed on other snakes.
- They are one of the four most deadly snakes in India.
- The venom of kraits is 15 times more deadly than that of the well-known cobra snake.
- As deadly as they are, they are quite calm and relaxed.
- They can be handled without biting; they become aggressive when over or mishandled.
- They like flat plains like rice dams and rice fields.
- They like to live near water bodies.
- They sometimes feed on their own young.

KEELBACK SNAKE

The keelback snake is the only semi-aquatic and non-venomous snake of Australia. The name keelback is gotten from the highly keeled scales of its body. The body is rough to the touch instead of being smooth. These keeled scales are the distinguishing feature of keelbacks.

Keelback snakes are harmless but resembles venomous snakes that have rough scales. Keelbacks are also known as water snake, swamp tiger, and freshwater snake.

Description and size:

They are very small snakes with an average length of 50 to 75 cm and maximum length of 1 meter. They are black or olive-brown in color. They also have a faint banded pattern.

Where they are found:

Keelback snakes are fond of damp places are often found close to freshwater like creeks dams and swamps.

They are found in Eastern and Northern Queensland, North-east New South Wales and Western Australia.

Behavior:

Keelbacks are active during the day and at night. They are able to grip onto slippery surfaces in mud and vegetation by using their keeled scales. When they are not moving, keelbacks like to hide timber, plants or in empty burrows.

What they eat and how they hunt for food:

Keelback snakes eat vertebrates like tadpoles, frogs, and lizards. They seize their preys using their sharp backward-curved teeth. Keelbacks swallow their preys from the rear, unlike other snakes that swallow the heads of their preys first. Their bodies are not that strong to fight the poisons in toad's skins, so they prefer to feed on small or medium-sized toads.

Reproduction

Their mating season begins in September. Keelbacks lay eggs. They produce between 5 and 12 eggs on average and can produce a maximum of 18 eggs.

Interesting facts about keelback snakes:

- They are harmless and will often release foul-smelling odor when firmly handled. The odor smells like a fart.
- Keelbacks are often mistaken for Eastern brown snakes because of their strong resemblance.
- They are more active in the warmer days.

- They are active during the day and at night.
- They like places with water like creeks and swamps. They are also found in parks, gardens, forests, pastures, heaths.

BLACK RAT SNAKE

The Black Rat Snake is also known as the Pilot Black Snake with no venom. They produce terrible smells when they have some type of threat around them, which is usually enough to get the problem to go away.

Description

An adult Black Rat Snake can be up to 8 feet in length. This makes them the biggest of all snakes found in Canada. Their colors allow them to blend well with the surroundings. Some are a dark gray or black color on top with white underneath depending on the types.

They have scales which makes it easier for them in climbing. They possessed a wedge-shaped head and large eyes. Their tail segments are also very long.

Distribution

They are found in North America. They tend to stick to areas that are heavily wooded. Both Texas and Nebraska have high numbers of them. There are also some living in areas of Wisconsin. In recent years they have been located in Oklahoma. The populations in Southern Canada and in New York are very small.

They have been found living at sea level, the highest regions of the Appalachians Mountains, and everything in between. They do well in trees, the water, on flat farm land, and even in rocky regions. There really isn't anywhere that they don't seem to be able to make into a home.

Behavior

1. They are good climbers, i.e. they possessed the ability to climb trees and mountains.
2. They also possess good swimming ability which enables them to get to various hunting locations with ease. They often freeze up when they feel startled and the body may kink in various places.
3. They are known to make sounds like Rattlesnakes too. It is believed that this is a way for them to wade off threats by deceit.

Diet /Feeding

The Black Rat Snakes are constrictors which coil around the bodies of their preys and cut off the abilities of the preys to breathe. They consume a wide variety of food including rodents, chipmunks, other snakes, and just about anything else they can find in their given habitat.

Reproduction

Their reproductive life includes;

1. The male has to wait for the female before mating occurs.
2. The males always involved in a serious fight for the right to be with females.
3. Once mating has occurred, each goes on their separate ways.
4. Once the female does lay its eggs, it takes about 70 days before they emerge.
5. One unique characteristic of the black rat snake is that their females don't cater for their young ones. They are born ready to care or themselves from the start. They will have to find shelter and food to survive. They are loners from the start, so these young don't stay with each other to try to figure it out. This is why there is a high rate of mortality among the Black Rat Snake offspring.

Danger to Humans

These snakes produce no venom but their smell maybe repulsive when moved close to. This can make you smell bad but nothing that a good shower won't take care of. They are constrictors but they aren't strong enough to coil around a human body and hold on to them tight enough to cut off airways.

CORN SNAKE

The Corn snake is also known as the Red Rat Snake. They are constrictor type of snakes, in other words, they wrap their bodies around what they want to eat or think is a threat. The name comes from the fact that they are often found around corn. They tend to feed more on rodents.

Some of them can be referred to as Jungle Corn Snakes. Some are more venomous and dangerous, depending on the parents.

Description

They can be up to 6 feet long and are very pretty. Their bodies have patterns of colors which make it easier for them to blend well with their surroundings. Some of them are orange with red lines down the sides while others may be black and their belly region is usually checkered in all of these colors.

Some of their colors may be determined by their surroundings which enable them to blend in and remain well hidden.

Distribution

North America is home to the Corn Snake. Just about anywhere that is warm and offers plenty of rodents is a good home for them. They tend to be around old buildings, farm ground, and they enjoy trees. They are mainly found on the ground but they have no problems with climbing. Texas and New Jersey are common locations for them to be found.

Behavior

The Corn Snake is one of the timidest you will find out there. Corn snakes are not known to bite humans. They always tend to hide when the weather is too cold for them but always out when the weather is warm.

Feeding

Almost all of the food for the Corn Snake comes from rodents. However, they can scale trees in order to reach bird eggs. They use their bodies to tightly constrict the prey until it can't breathe anymore. The young often starts out by dining on lizards.

Reproduction

The female starts with the reproduction process by giving off a strong smell which will encourage the male to come to look for her so that mating can take place. The female will lay her eggs about 1 month after mating has taken place. She will find a place that is warm and moist for them to be incubated. She can have up to 24 eggs. Once she lays them, she will leave them. They will emerge about 10 weeks later using a tooth that can get through the tough leathery shell. A Corn Snake may live from 5 to 8 years in the wild.

Danger to Humans

Due to the lovely colors of the Corn Snake and the fact that they don't bite often they are one of the most popular types people keep for pets. Should you be bitten by one, it is best to get it looked at by a doctor because some people have an allergic reaction.

ATHERIS

Atheris is popularly known as bush vipers. They are found only in tropical sub-Saharan Africa and many species have Isolated and fragmented distributions due to their confinement to the rain forest. They are similar to the arboreal pit vipers of Asia and South America.

Description

They are relatively small in size, with adults ranging in total length from 40 cm (16 in) to a maximum of 78 cm (31 in). All species have a broad, triangular head that is distinct from the neck. Their canthus is also distinct and the snout is broad. The crown is covered with small imbricate or smooth scales, none of which is enlarged.

Distribution

They are found in tropical sub-Saharan Africa, excluding southern Africa. Some species have only isolated populations, surviving in small sections of ancient rainforest.

Habitat

They inhabit rainforest regions, mostly in remote areas far from human activity.

Behavior

All species are strictly arboreal, although they can sometimes be found on or near the ground.

Diets

Atheris species have been known to prey upon a variety of
small amphibians, lizards, rodents, birds, and even   other
snakes.

Reproduction

All atheris species are ovoviviparous. Mating takes place in
September-November and the females give birth to live young
in March-April.

Venom

Their venom is strongly hemotoxic, causing pain, swelling and
blood clotting problems. Their venom has recently been
regarded as less toxic than that of many other species.

BLIND SNAKES

Blind snakes are a family of nonvenomous snakes mostly found in Asia and Africa. These snakes have been introduced into many parts of the world. They like to burrow into the soil. They have the appearance and habits of earthworms, which is why most people mistake them for earthworms. They have scales and a very shiny body. They are the most widespread land snakes in the world. They are a unisexual species of snakes, i.e. there are only females and no males.

They have small bodies which are covered in smooth and shiny black scales. They have rigid skulls and eyes.

One of their alternative names, flowerpot snakes is gotten from the fact that they are introduced to many parts of the world by attaching themselves to potted plants like flowers and are moved from where they are originally located to other areas of the world.

Description and size

Adult blind snakes are thin and small with an average length of between 6 and 18 cm. The tail and the head look alike. The scales on their heads are small and look like those on the body. They have colors of purple, silver gray and charcoal gray.

Their very small eyes are covered with scales, making them almost totally blind except that they can see light.

Where they are found

They are found originally in Asia (Iran, Nepal, Pakistan, India, Sri Lanka, the Maldives, Bangladesh, Singapore, Vietnam, China, Taiwan, Hong Kong, etc.) and Africa (Senegal, Togo, Ivory Coast,

South Africa, Cameroon, Tanzania, Mozambique, Madagascar, Seychelles, etc.) but have been introduced to other parts of the world like America (USA: Texas, California, Louisiana, Florida, and Massachusetts; Mexico; Cayman Islands; and Guatemala), Australia (Queensland Darwin), and Oceania (Fiji, Palau, Guam, etc.).

They live in agricultural and urban areas. They live underground in termite and ant nests. They can also be found under moist leaves, logs, dry jungle, city gardens, and in the wet forest.

What they eat and how they hunt for food
They feed on the eggs, pupae, and larvae of termites and ants. They live for the most part in undergrounds and come to the surface in search of food or after heavy rain.

When threatened, they sometimes release a foul-smelling chemical.

Blind snakes are prey to a lot of animals like mammals, birds, fishes, snakes, and spiders. They also occasionally eat centipedes and millipedes.

When searching for food, blind snakes will trail and go after ants using chemicals released by them. They will follow them to their nests where they will feed on any ant found there. Their tight and overlapping scales protect them from the stings and bites of ants.

Reproduction
Blind snakes are a unisexual species composed only of females and no male. They can either give birth to live young or lay

eggs. They reproduce by the process of parthenogenesis, i.e. production of unfertilized eggs which later hatch and look exactly like the mother. They have a short incubation period. They produce around 8 offsprings. All the produced baby snakes are female. They can easily give birth to young ones without having to look for mates.

Interesting facts about blind snakes

- They are widely distributed. They are the most widely distributed land snakes.
- They are easily mistaken for earthworms.
- They have teeth on only the upper or lower jaw.
- They sometimes cut their prey into several parts before eating them.
- They can climb trees.
- They sometimes guard their eggs.
- They are very small, like the size of a penny.
- They are all females and no males
- They may look like earthworms but are not segmented.
- They cannot shorten and lengthen their bodies the way earthworms can.

Green Snake

Green snakes also are known as green grass snakes or grass snakes are a family of slender, nonvenomous, docile, small, and green colored snakes. They either have smooth dorsal scales or rough dorsal scales.

They are non-aggressive snakes and can be approached by humans. When threatened by humans, they often run away. They hardly bite and when they do; they have no venom.

They are found in North America. They live in open woods, in marshes, along the edges of streams, and meadows.

They mate from spring to summer and lay eggs around June to September.

Description and size

The green snakes have a   white or yellow colored bellies and bright or light green colored backs. They are of small-medium size, i.e. their sizes are between small and large. Their average lengths are between 36 and 51 cm as adults. Their tails take up about half or a quarter of their total lengths. Male green snakes have longer tails than the females.

Baby green snakes have olive green, brown or blue-gray colored backs but change to bright green as they mature.

They have round and large eyes. They also use their tongues to smell their surroundings.

Where they are found

They are found in Canada, Northern Mexico, Wisconsin, Maine, Virginia, Colorado, Texas, Utah, Mississippi, Missouri, Kansas, Iowa, Wyoming, Illinois, Indiana, and New Jersey.

Behavior

They often live near water and are very good swimmers. They are highly arboreal. They like to climb low vegetation. They also live on the ground. They are mostly active during the day. They like to stay near green vegetation for camouflage. They like to lie in the sun on logs and rocks so as to raise their body temperature.

When threatened, they run away and they can also release a foul-smelling chemical from their bodies.

What they eat and how they hunt for food

They mostly feed on insects and spiders. They also eat tree frogs, snails, moths, worms, slugs, ants and caterpillars.

Green snakes will use their eyes, tongues, and chemicals to search for prey. They do not inject venom into their prey or wrap around them like constrictor snakes; they will simply grab and swallow them alive.

Predation

Predators of green snakes are other snakes like the eastern king snake, the eastern racer, birds like the great blue heron, the red-tailed hawk, bears, foxes, raccoons, and cats.

Reproduction

They breed in spring and in fall. Female green snakes lay between 2 and 14 eggs. They lay eggs under boards, under a rock, under tree barks, in deep mulch, in burrows of rodents, piles of sawdust, rotting logs and mounds of rotting vegetation.

Their eggs are oval and white. Eggs hatch between 4 and 23 days after they are laid.

Interesting facts about green snakes

- They are excited and calm down when handled by humans.
- They have no ears and rely on vibrations to know their surroundings.
- They shed their skins as often as once in 4 or 5 weeks
- They like to use burrows of rodents and ant hills as part-time homes during hibernation.
- Human beings like to keep them as pets.
- They are also sold by humans for their nice skin and passive nature.
- They don't survive well in captivity.
- The use of pesticides is greatly affecting the population of green snakes.
- States like Indiana, Iowa, Missouri, North Carolina, Michigan, Montana, Texas, Wyoming, Colorado, and Nebraska have made laws to protect the green snakes. These laws are against the collection of green snakes for individual or commercial use.

CAT SNAKE

The cat snakes are a family of nocturnal species of snakes. They are agile and active hunters and are capable of climbing rocks and trees to search for prey like lizards, bats, rodents and fledglings. While hunting, they like to sneak up on their prey, strike them and release venom into their body.

They are non-aggressive but venomous snakes. They are not dangerous to humans.

They are scattered throughout the world except for Antarctica.

Their name is gotten from the shape and size of their eyes and pupils. They have small eyes and elliptical or vertical pupils which gives them the appearance of cats, hence the name cat snakes.

Description and size

They have a large head and greenish-grey or reddish-brown eyes and vertical pupils making them look like vipers. The body is colored reddish-brown or reddish-grey with banded markings. They have a set of venomous fangs at the back of their upper jaws. Their average body size is 70 cm but they can grow to a size of 130 cm.

Where they are found

They are scattered all over the dry regions of the world from Africa to Europe, Asia, South America, North America, and Australia, except Antarctica.

They are found on mountains and hills, both semi-arid and arid regions but are absent from open desert.

Venom / Bite

They are known to be mildly venomous and are not dangerous to human beings. They seldom bite and rarely release their venom in defensive bites. When bit, the person will most likely experience minor swelling and local pain and will only lead to an infection when it's not properly treated, but not death.

What they eat and how they source for food

They feed mainly on lizards, small geckos, birds, frogs, toads, tadpoles and small mammals. They also feed on the eggs of these animals. Baby cat snakes feed on invertebrates.

Their mild venom is not used to kill the prey but is actually used to relax the body of the prey so that cat snakes can overpower them.

Reproduction

They are oviparous snakes, i.e. their females lay eggs. Their eggs are laid in clutches of between 5 and 9 eggs. The eggs hatch in either late summer or early autumn.

Interesting facts about cat snake

- They mostly live in dry places but can be found in residential areas close to where humans live.
- They are great climbers and can climb walls and trees.
- They have short tails.
- They possess slender bodies.
- Their body color varies with that of their surroundings to provide them with camouflage.
- They are nocturnal snakes
- They are shy, calm and difficult to understand.
- They also feed on other snakes.
- Because of their similarity to venomous species of snakes such as the vipers, cat snakes are often killed by humans.

GLOSSARY

Arboreal: Used to refer to something relating to or resembling a tree. Also of a habitat which means animals are living in or among trees.

Artheris: Also known as the bush viper, they are snake species predominant to tropical sub-Sahara in Africa

Adders: An old English word which means serpent. Used to refer to a particular group of venomous snakes which are not totally dangerous to man.

Amphibians: Vertebrate animals that don't bear amniotic eggs and live on both land and in water. |Also used to mean that something has two natures.

Amphibious: Having the characteristics of amphibians.

Anaconda: A snake of genus *Eunectus* found mainly in Northern South America, and is largely nonvenomous.

Black Mamba: The second largest venomous snake in the world. It is usually fast, highly aggressive, nervous and lethally venomous

Black Rat Snake: Also known as Pilot Black Snake, it is a nonvenomous snake that produces a terrible and repulsive smell once it sights threats around it. Its long body makes it the biggest of snakes found in Canada

Blind snakes: Easily mistaken for earthworms with their looks and small bodies which are covered in smooth and shiny black scales with rigid skulls and eyes, they are a member of the non-venomous snakes, mostly found in Asia and Africa

Cat snake: This is a snake that belongs to the nocturnal species of snakes. It is an agile as well as active hunter capable of climbing heights to search for preys. It is non-aggressive but a venomous snake.

Camouflage: Resemblance of an organism to its surroundings in a bid to avoid detection, hence avoiding getting preyed.

Carnivorous: Characteristic of carnivores. Used to mean than an animal feeds largely on the flesh of other animals.

Chrysopelea: Gliding snake, more commonly referred to as flying snake which belongs to the family of mildly venomous snakes.

Cobra: Any of the various venomous snake of the family *Elapidae.*

Constrictors: Snakes that squeeze their prey to kill them.

Cottonmouth: Also called water moccasin, black moccasin, water mamba, black snake, water pilot, mangrove rattler.

Corn snake: Also known as Red Rat snake, it is a constrictor type of snake whose name came from corn because they are always seen around it.

Copperhead: Used to refer to snakes having a copper-colored head.

Coyotes: Species of canine (*canis latrans*) native to North America.

Den: A small cavern or hollow place inside of a hill or among rocks, especially a cave used by a snake for shelter or concealment.

Desert: An arid or dry land having no water or vegetation.

Diurnal: Used to represent animals that are active during daylight.

Enzyme: A globular protein mostly biochemical substances that catalyzes biochemical reactions in plants and animals.

Equator: An imaginary line which is equidistant from the two poles of the earth and dividing the earth surface into the northern and southern hemisphere.

Fang: That feature on a snake's body which grasps, captures, seizes and holds its prey.

Garter snake: This is used to represent any of the various nonvenomous snakes of the genus *Thamnophis*, native to America with longitudinal stripes.

Hemotoxic: Causing toxicity, pains and swelling in blood flowing regions, thus resulting in blood clotting problems.

Hibernate: Sometimes called aestivation, it is a period of inactivity as experienced by living organisms.

Incubation: Sitting on eggs for the purpose of hatching young, brooding on, or keeping warm to develop the life within by any process.

Incubation Period: The period of time within which living organisms, most especially the egg-laying ones, sit on the egg to hatch them.

Krait: Commonly known as blue krait, it is one of the four most venomous snakes in India.

Keelback: A nonvenomous and semi-aquatic snake original to Australia.

Mammals: These are animals characterized with mammary gland, hair on their skin and most importantly, give birth to their young ones alive.

Mating: The process of copulation involving male and female organisms.

Meadow: A piece of land covered or cultivated with grass, usually intended to be mown for hay. It is usually an area of low-lying vegetation, especially near a river.

Mongoose: Carnivore of a particular animal family famed as a predator of venomous snakes

Neurotoxins: The venom released by during cobra's bite that affects the human nervous system.

Nocturnal: Relating to animals that are active in darkness or in the night.

Nonvenomous: Having no venom.

Ophiophagus: A characteristic possessed by snake to predate on snakes.

Oviparous: Having the capacities to lay eggs

Ovoviviparous: Relating to reptiles and animals whose eggs hatch within their body.

Predator: Any animal that hunt, attack and kill another organism primarily for food.

Prey: An animal that is eaten up or attacked by other organisms.

Python: A particular type of large constricting snake.

Play fighting: The attitude put up by male snakes to attract its female counterpart reproductively.

Raccoons: A nocturnal omnivore native to North America typically with a mixture of gray, brown and black fur, a mask-like marking around the eyes, and a stripped tail.

Rattle: A sound made by loose objects, usually shaking or vibrating against one another.

Rattlesnake: Any of the various poisonous American snakes of genera *Crotalus* and *Sistrurus*, having a rattle at the end of its tail.

Reptiles: A vertebrate organism of the class reptilian creeping on its belly or by means of small and short legs.

Segment: Divisions and sections of a living organism which majorly allows for easy naming and identification.

Snake: A legless reptile of the class *Serpents* usually with a long, thin body and a fork-shaped tongue.

Snout: Of or relating to the nose. A projecting nose, mouth, and jaw of an animal.

Specie: Used mostly to distinguish and classify animal or having to with a particular group of animals.

Venom: A poison usually carried by a snake and injected to the enemy or prey by a sting or bite.

INDEX